EAT CAKE
FOR BREAKFAST
AND 99 OTHER
SMALL ACTS
OF HAPPINESS

Written and illustrated by
Viola Sutanto

ISBN: 978-1-951412-16-6

LCCN: 2020915630

Manufactured in China.

Design by Viola Sutanto.

10 9 8 7 6 5 4 3 2 1

The Collective Book Studio
Oakland, California
www.thecollectivebook.studio

Dedicated to Maika & Alistair,
the two most courageous kids
I have ever loved.

introduction

"Life is not measured by the number of
breaths we take, but by the moments that
take our breath away."
~Anonymous

"Are you happy?" Ask a kid this simple question and you'll
probably get an unequivocal "Yes!" Adults, on the other
hand, are often befuddled and likely will answer the question
with another question like, "Do you mean, like now?"
Or you might get a response such as, "Well, kinda but I will
be happier once..."

I never thought much about this until I became a parent:
the universal craving for happiness and how hard we work
to achieve it as adults.

Happiness felt like a grand concept, a lofty ideal to be
achieved after years of hard work, success, (insert your

criteria here) and when the stars are aligned. It was like the coveted prize at the finish line.

But what if you didn't have to wait for that perfect moment? What if happiness could be achieved every day, and through small, simple acts? What if each and every one of us could help spread a little joy every day?

A year ago, our 9-year-old daughter, Maika, was diagnosed with a rare, life-threatening blood disease called aplastic anemia, also known as bone marrow failure. Miraculously, our then 3-year-old son, Alistair, was a perfect match for her, so he became her bone marrow donor and saved her life.

During the months of her treatment, I was blown away by Maika's courage and positivity. This was the biggest fight of her life, and it was long and arduous, both physically and mentally. Yet, this little girl managed to find something to be happy about every single day she was in the hospital. Whether it was Nutella bagels for breakfast, or discovering re-runs of *Full House* on the hospital TV, or busting my butt at UNO, Maika found joy every day in the most challenging time of her life.

During our stay in the hospital, I started capturing these little moments of positivity. Initially, it was just a distraction, something to keep my hands busy during those long days. Over time, these drawing sessions became something we looked forward to doing together. From backyard picnics to wrapping dumplings and swinging at the playground, each sketch became a tiny sliver of hope; an activity she could once again enjoy when she got home.

Eat Cake for Breakfast and 99 Other Small Acts of Happiness is the culmination of these small joys every day. Even though this book was inspired by a little girl's journey to recovery, it's for anyone who needs a lift to get through the day. It's a book about finding what fills your soul, and doing more of it. It's a book you keep by your bedside, and a book you gift to your best friend, or your grandma.

May you always find light at the end of the tunnel.

xoxo
Viola

Small Acts
of Happiness
are ...

sharing a fresh loaf

waiting for the first pour

taking A
yoga class

Surprising a friend with a plant

Hiking A New trail

Writing love letters

Floating in a pool

Waving to your neighbor

♥ Hi!

Rediscovering old books

A-OK!

ASSURING a FRIEND

Slicing a fresh loaf

Going camping

listening to the chirping of birds

Packing a Backyard picnic

Looking at the same moon
5,000 miles apart

making freshly squeezed lemonade

Savoring Shorts Weather

Eating cake for Breakfast...

or lunch or Dinner

Running in new Shoes

Shaking a bowl of noodles

Making A Bouquet

Adopting a pet

Indulging in "ME" time

kayaking at dusk

making homemade s'mores

Going on a roadtrip

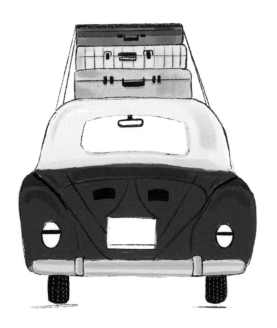

wearing striped pajamas...

and a
matching
beanie

Buying a New toothBrush

Stashing Nutella Packs

Skipping Stones

Sewing gifts for Friends

loading up on popcorn and Netflix

Building A Fort

planting something

Watching movies at the Drive-in

trying on a New lipStick

looking at clouds

INdulging iN EsseNtial oils

Picking Peaches

Brightening up the day
with fresh blooms

inviting a friend over

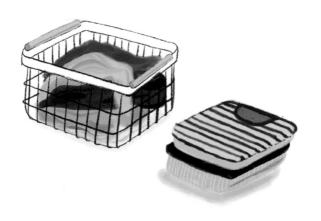

folding laundry

Catching Fireflies

binge-watching reruns

Eating tHat last
slice of pizza

Writing thank-you notes

painting rocks

Chilling by yourself

taking a long soak

GEttiNg takeOut

reading in bed

Celebrating small wins

Solving puzzles

SUPERSIZING THE FRIES

Shopping at the farmer's market

taking POWER NapS

Cleaning out your inbox
(even if only for a day)

Sharpening all your pencils

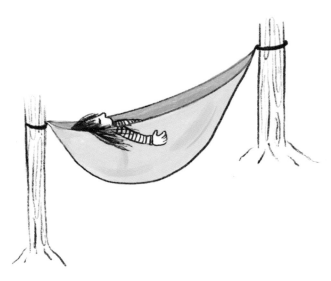

Napping in a hammock

Flipping through old photos

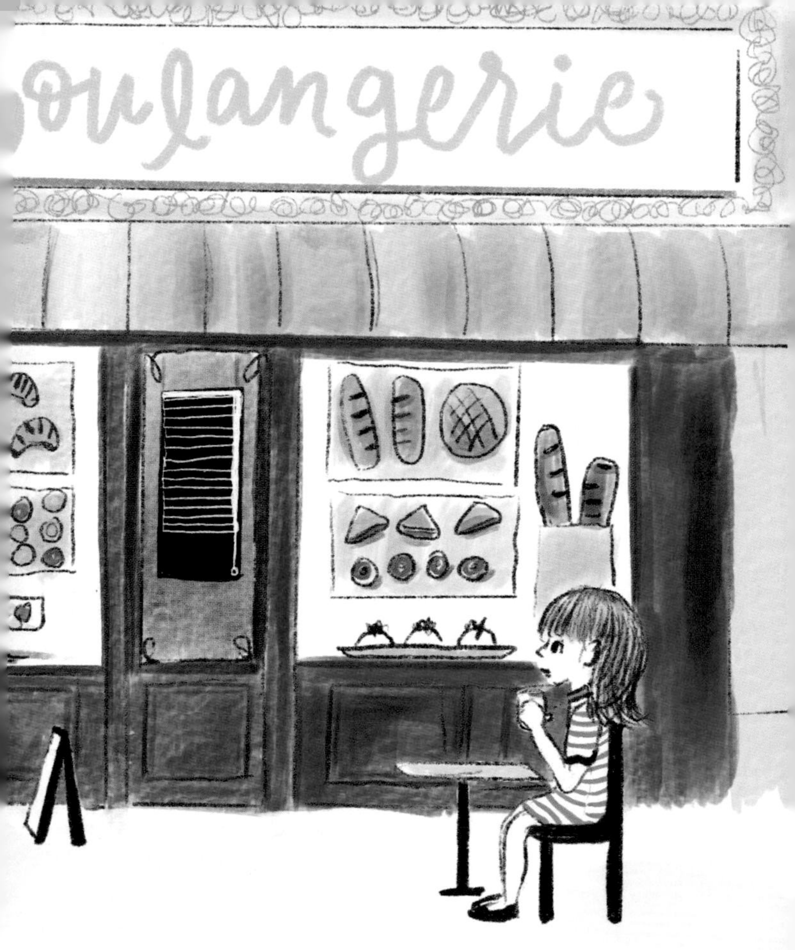

Watching the SunRiSe

Marie-kondoing your sock drawer

taking

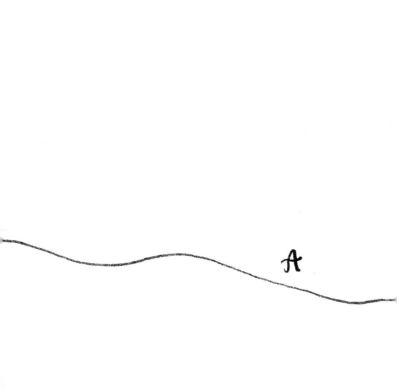

loooong

walk

Checking off that last to-do

Mending Something

Making Sandcastles

Napping with the windows open

Sitting quietly by a Stream

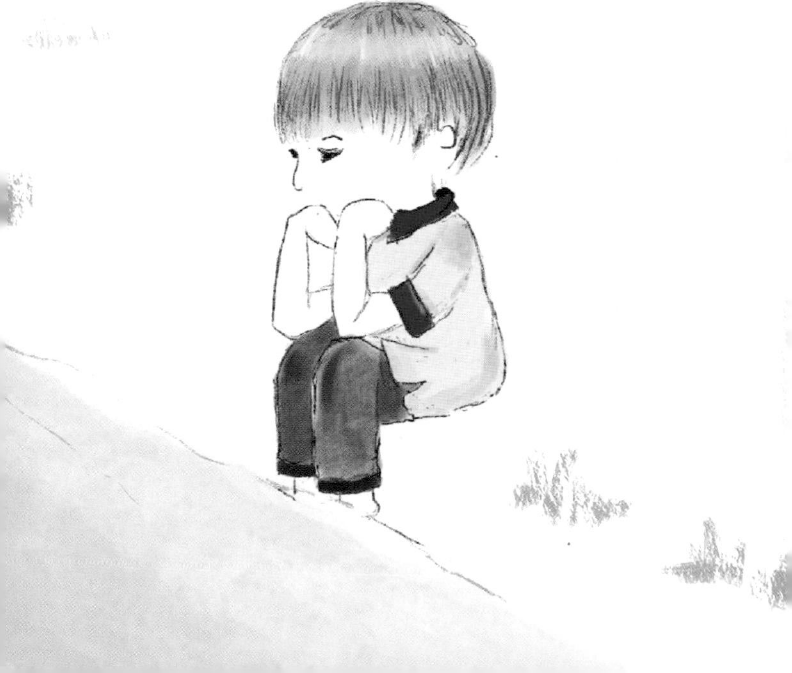

Picking up A NEW Skill

Adding Sprinkles

Getting Fresh Air

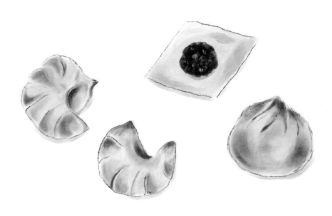

wrapping dumplings

twinning

Checking in on loved ones

Baking Brownie Cupcakes

taking DEEP BreathS

Donating unused items

making Smoothies

listening to the waves

Building A Snowman

SENDING A CARE PACKAGE

Sharing an umbrella

Skipping Rope

Collecting fall leaves

trying out a NEW RECIPE

warming frosty Hands

tipping generously

Planning Adventures

Apologizing first

NATATION
means swimming

ETUI is
a small
ornamental
case.

??

MOUSE POTATO
is someone who spends
tons of time on a computer.

MONKEY'S
WEDDING
means rain
AND sunshine at
the same time!

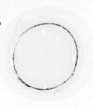

MERRYTHOUGHT
is the wishbone
of a BIRD!

LEARNING NEW WORDS

HONGI is a Maori greeting
where people press
their noses together.

HALLUX is
your big toe.

ENJOYING A SUNDAE

Working up a good Sweat

Riding the FERRIS WHEEL

RELEASING BALLOONS

midNight SNacKiNg

Sending good vibes

Swinging and thinking

Singing in the Shower

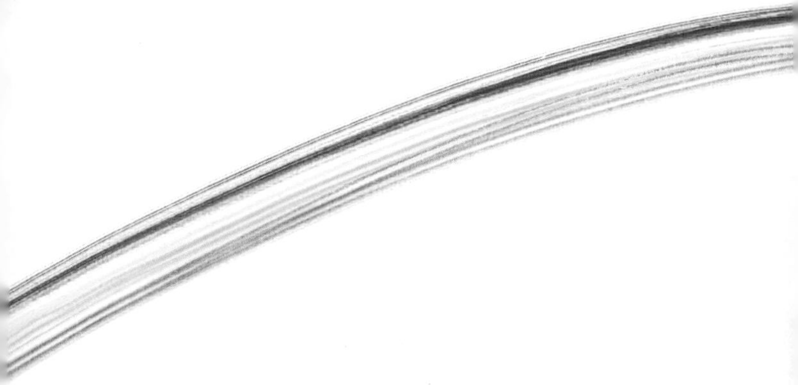

looking for
rainbows after
the storm

"If you take the little things
for granted, you lose the joy
in your life."

~Maika Ting, age 10

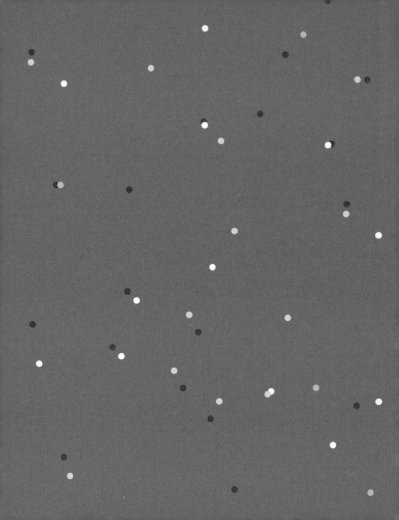